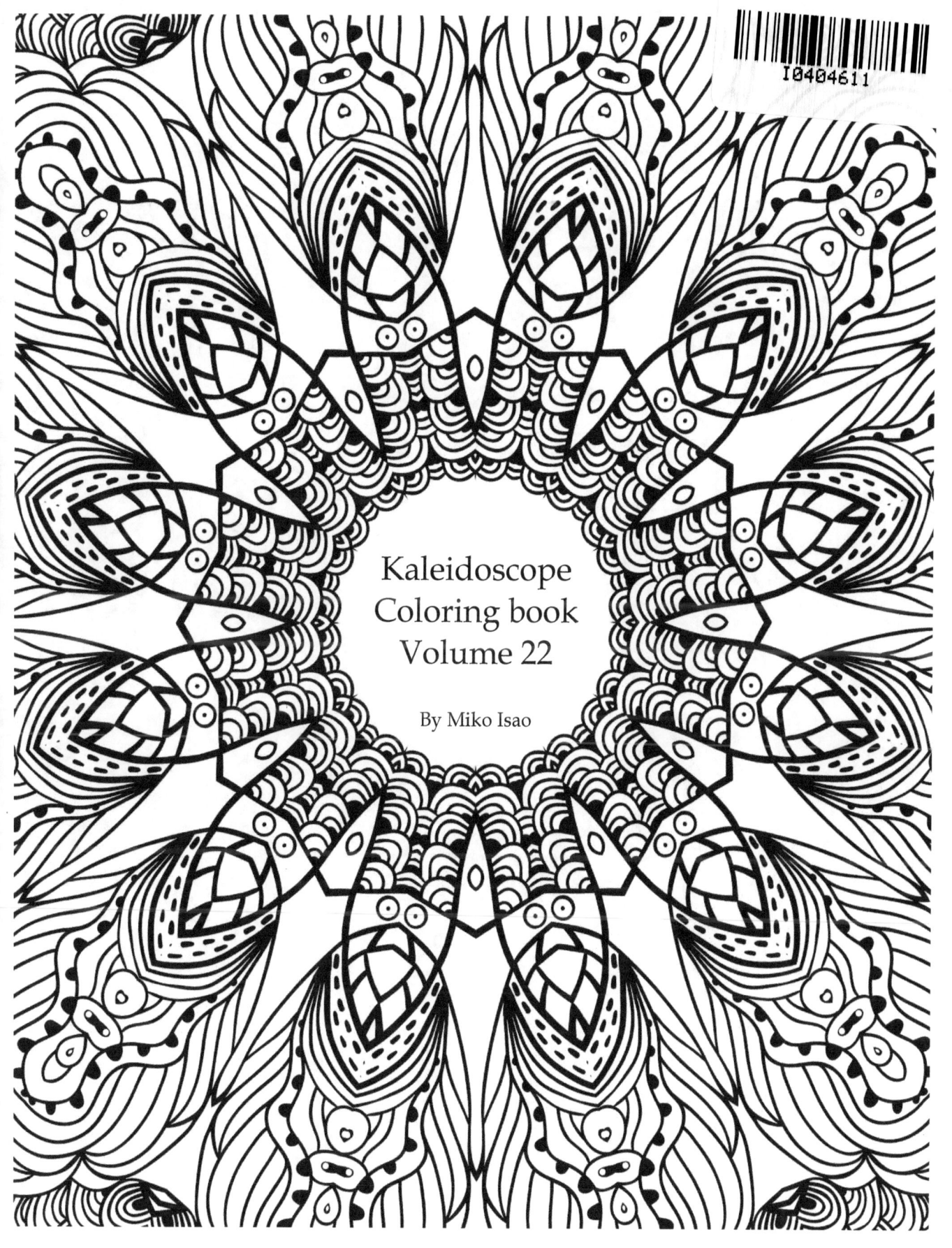

Kaleidoscope Coloring book (Volume 22)
A flowers, Mehdi, tattoo inspired for design and coloring

Copyright: Published in the United States by Miko Isao
Published September 2016

All rights reserved. No part of this publication may be reproduced, stored in retrieval system, copied in any form or by any means, electronic, mechanical, photocopying, recording or otherwise transmitted without written permission from the publisher. Please do not participate in or encourage piracy of this material in any way. You must not circulate this book in any format. Miko Isao does not control or direct users' actions and is not responsible for the information or content shared, harm and/or actions of the book readers.

ISBN-13: 978-1537753959
ISBN-10:1537753959

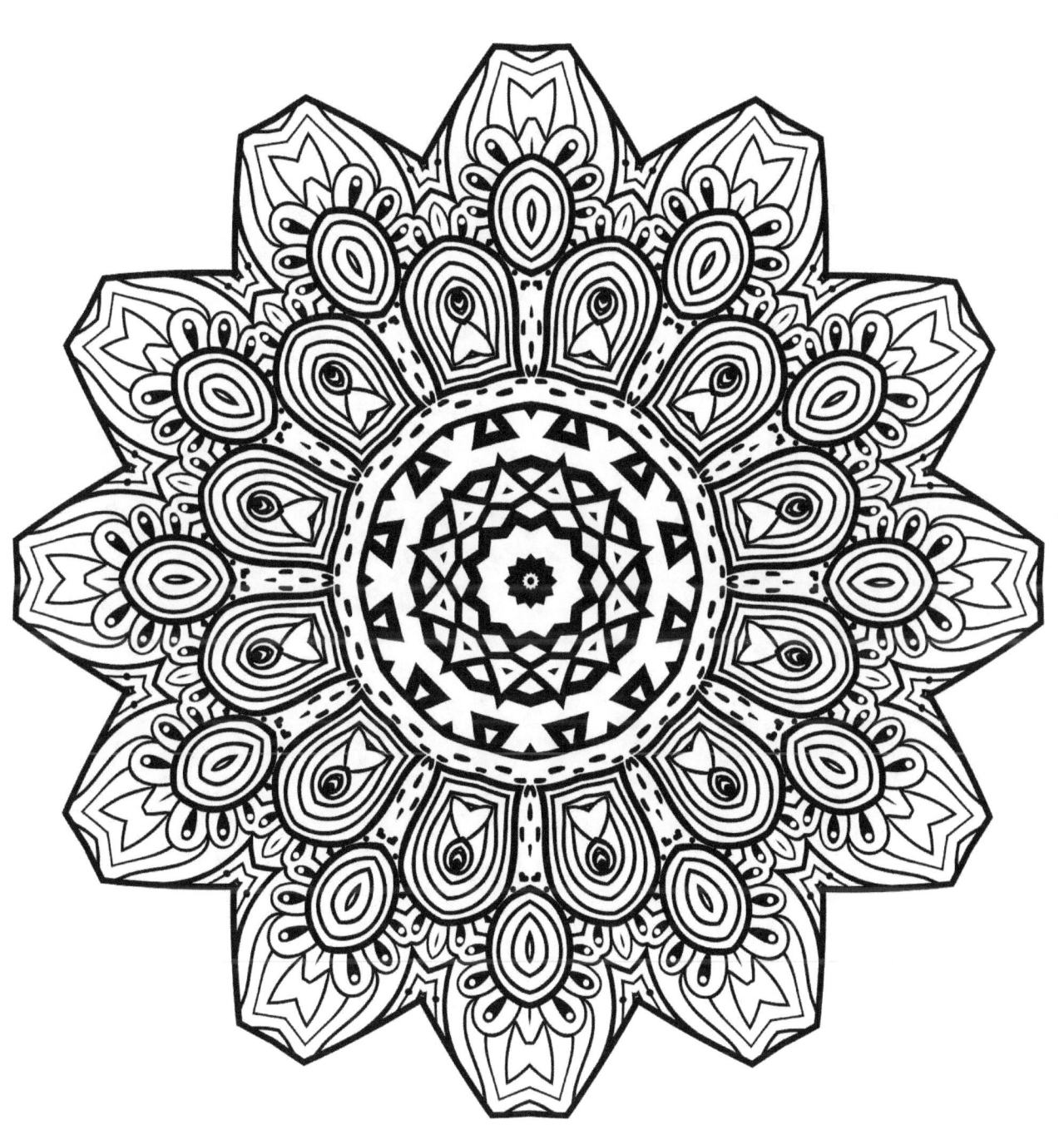

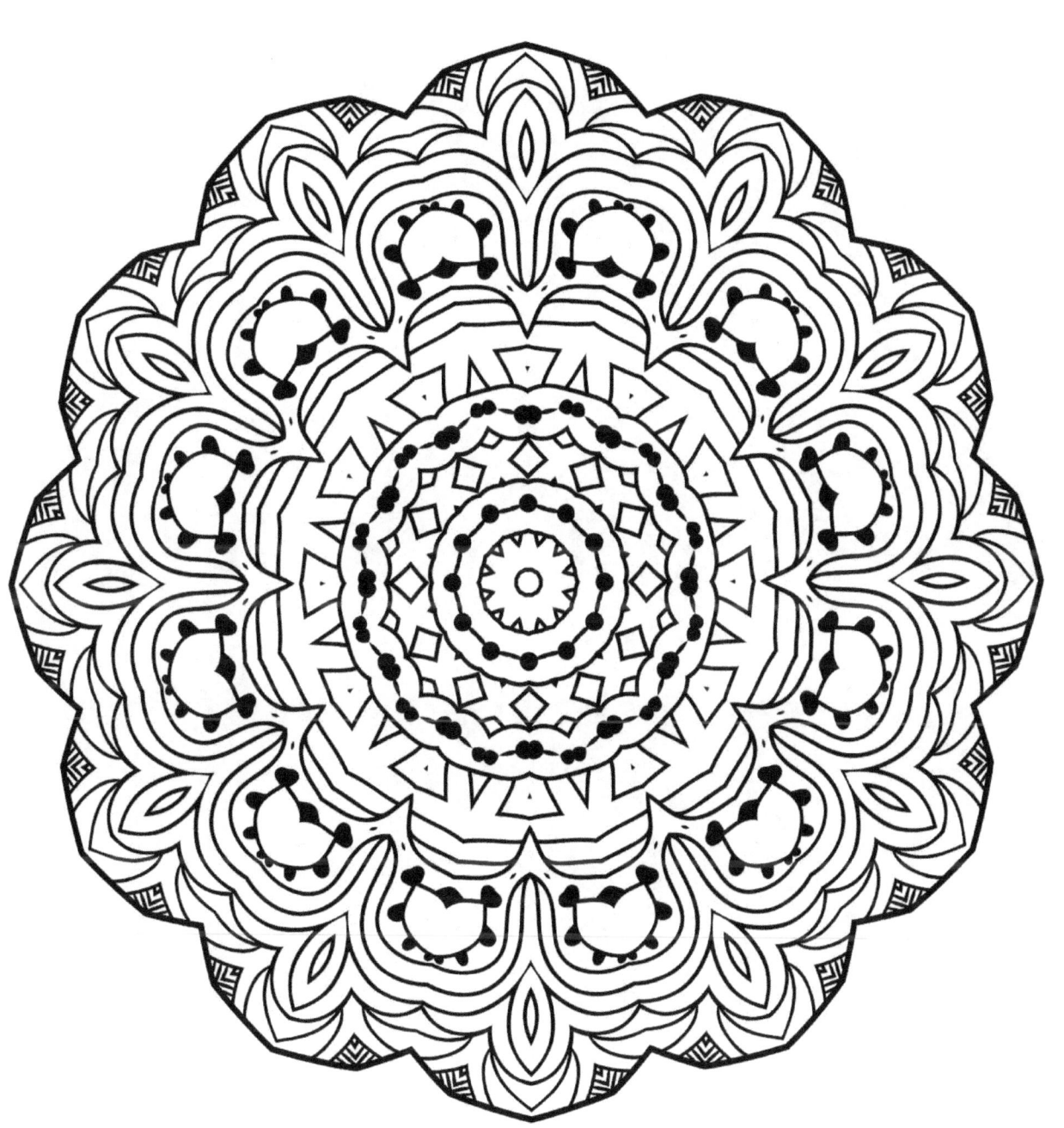

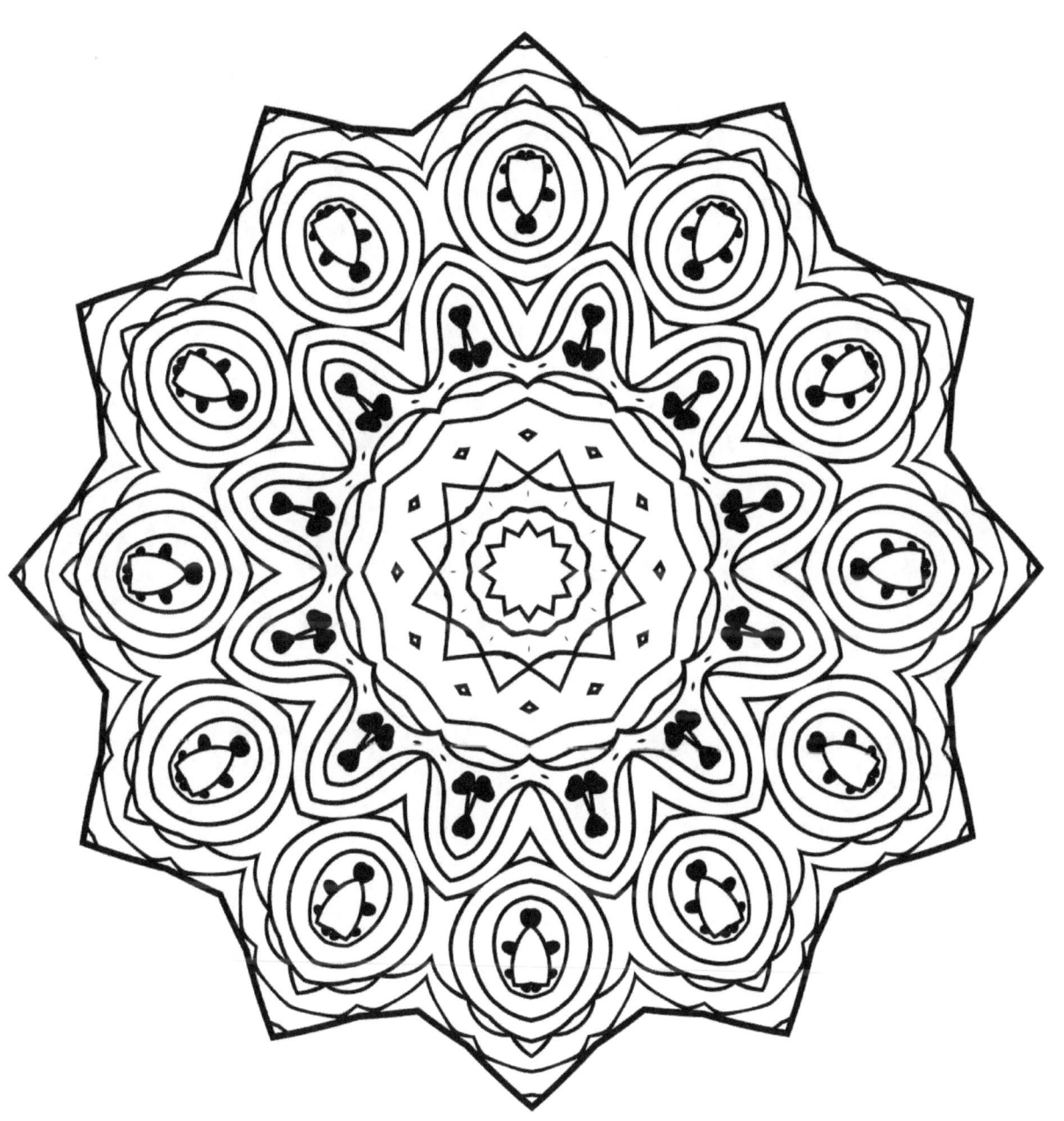

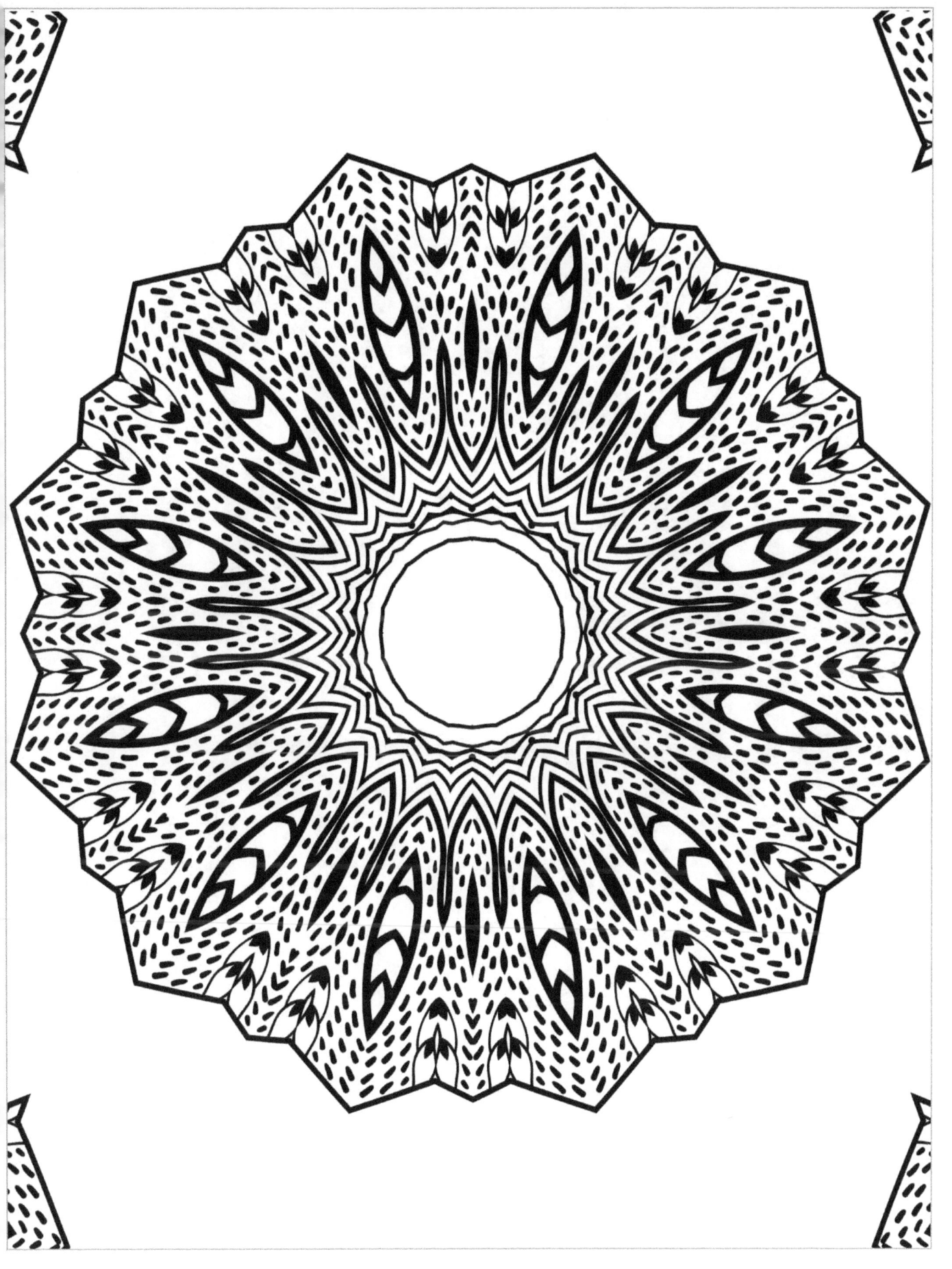

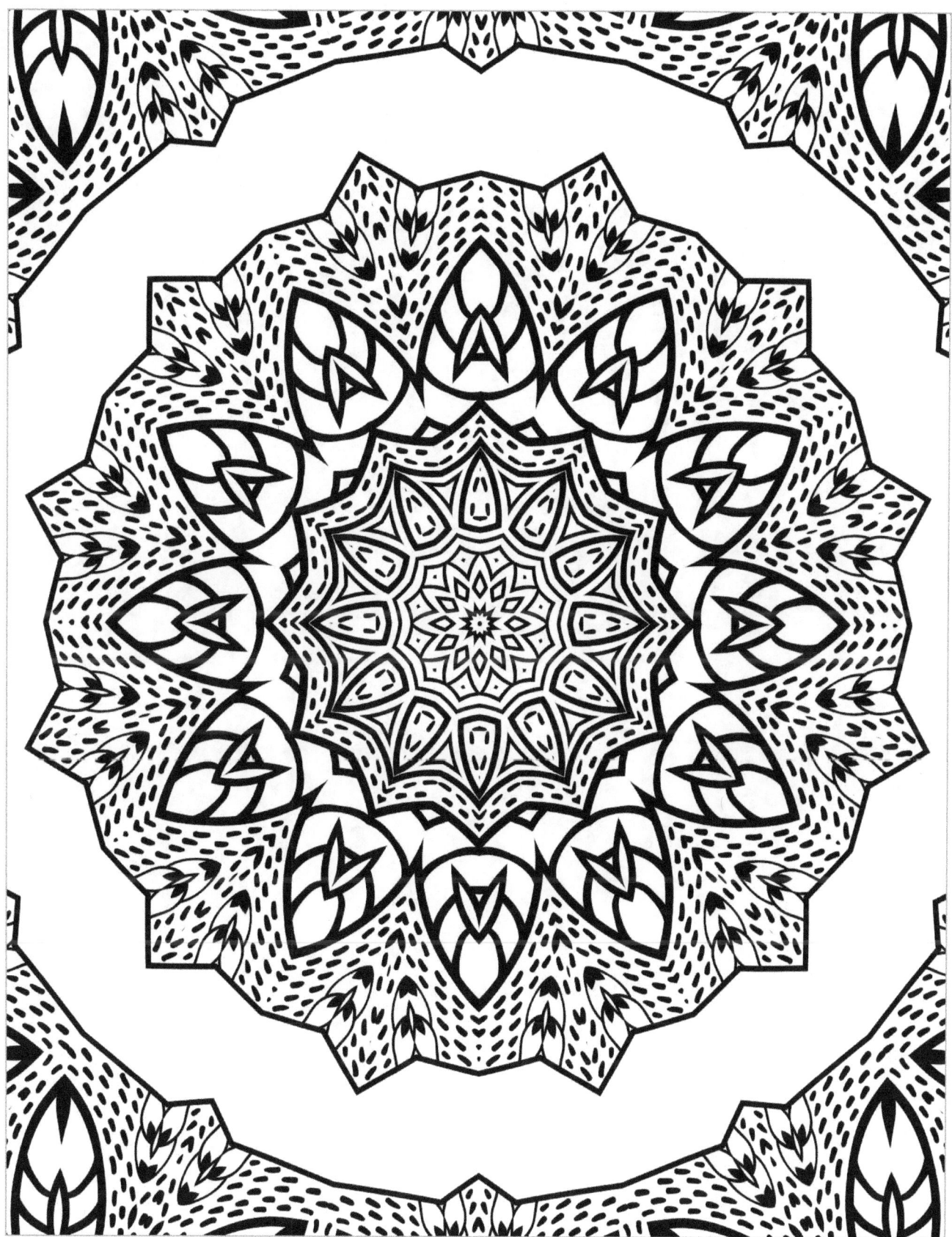

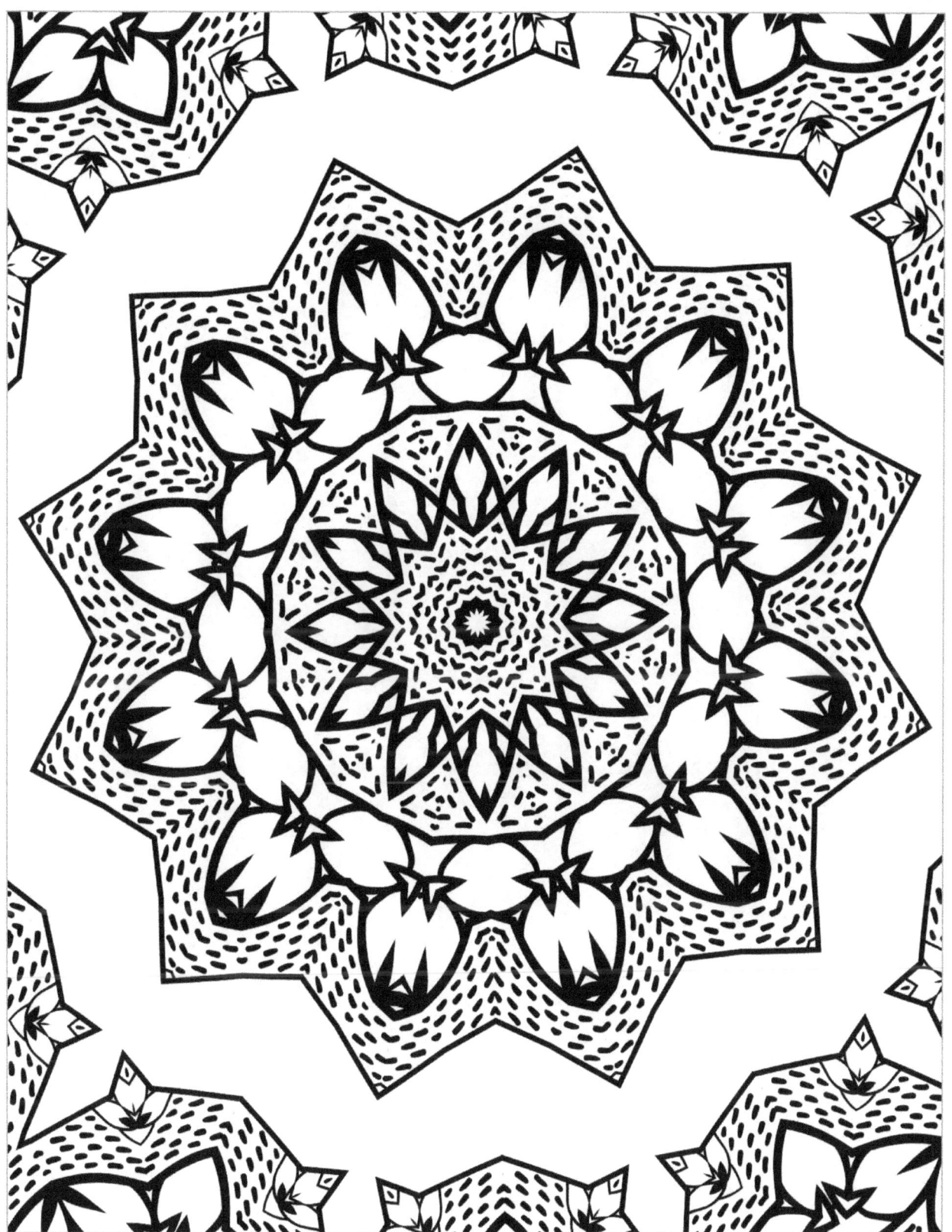

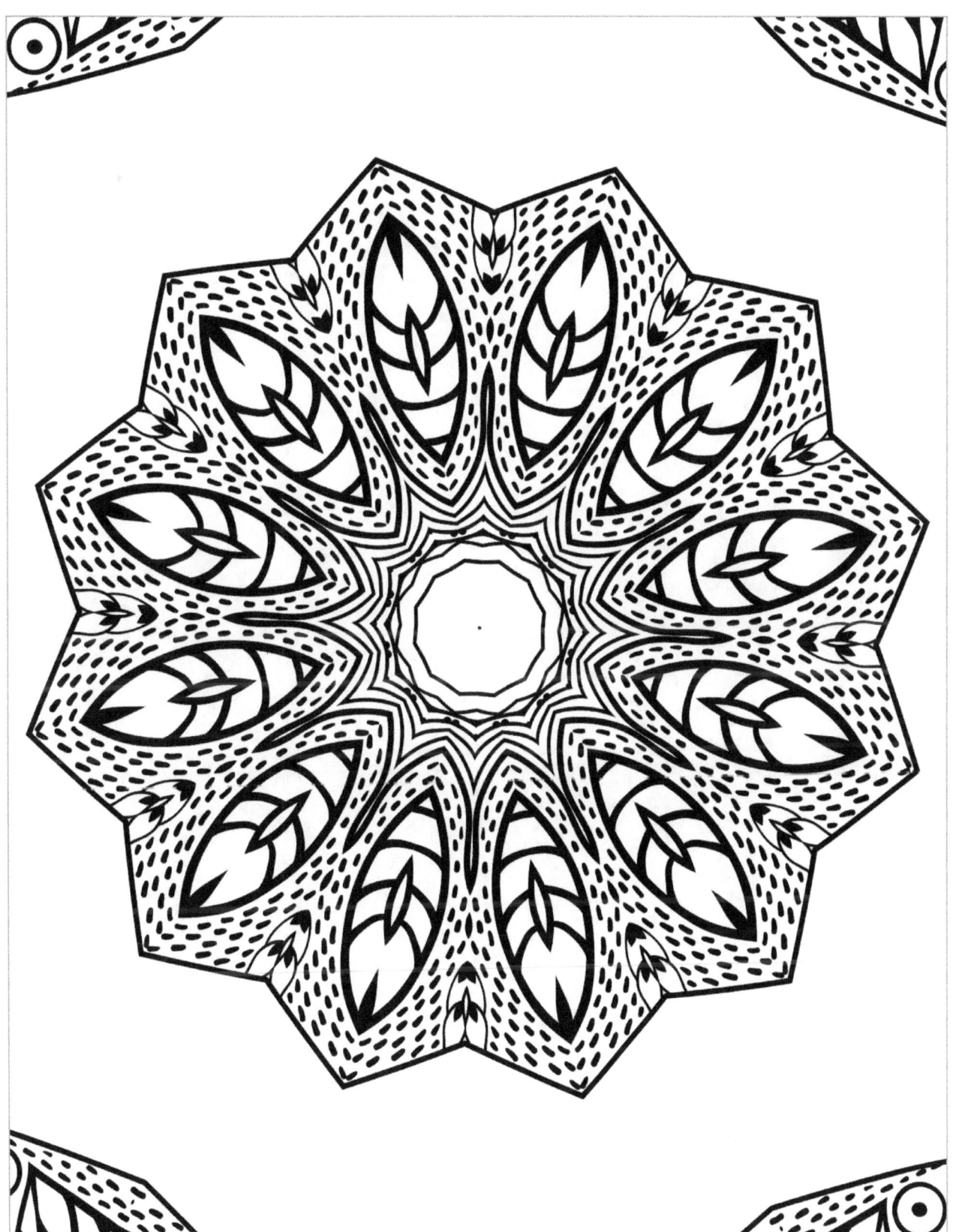

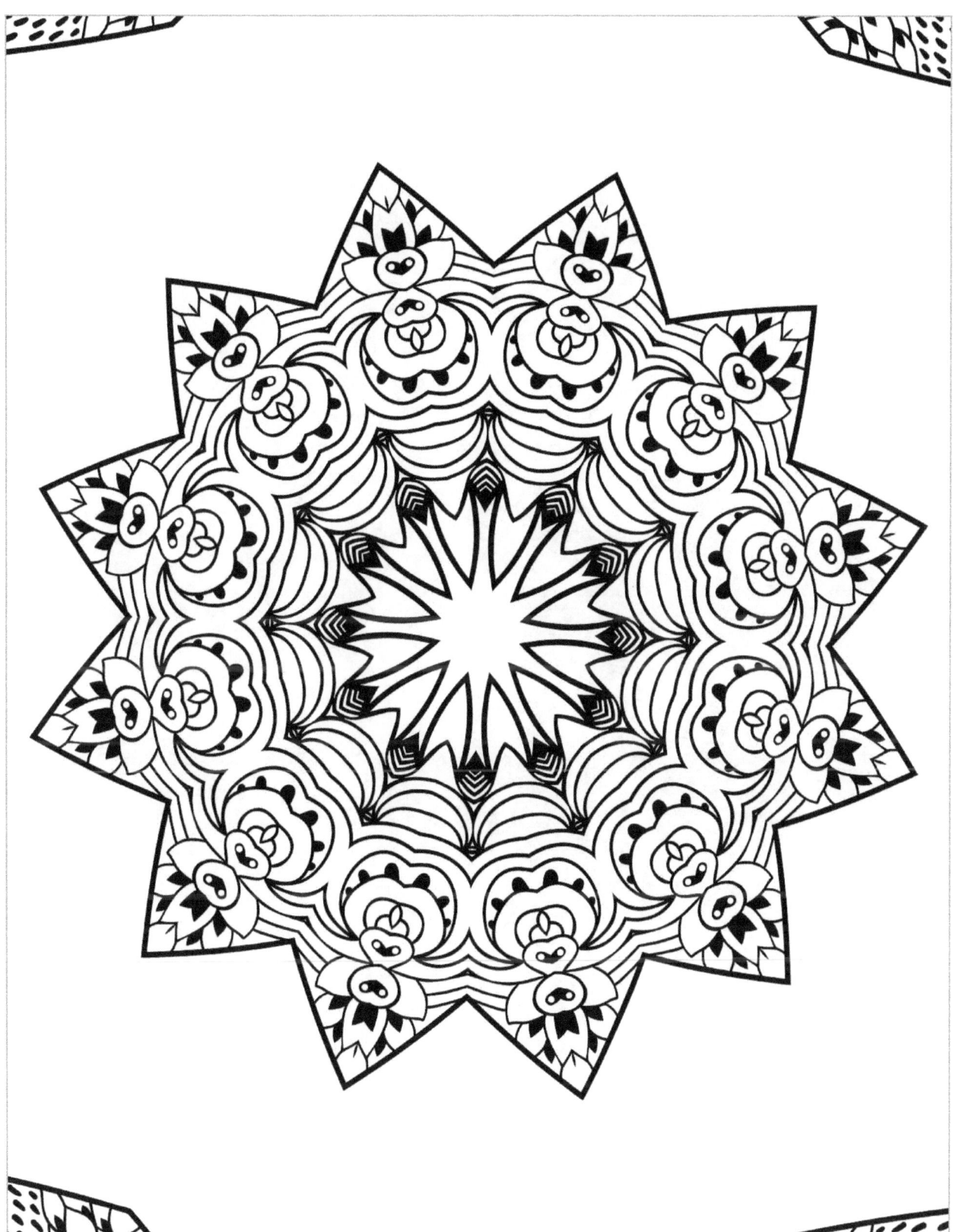

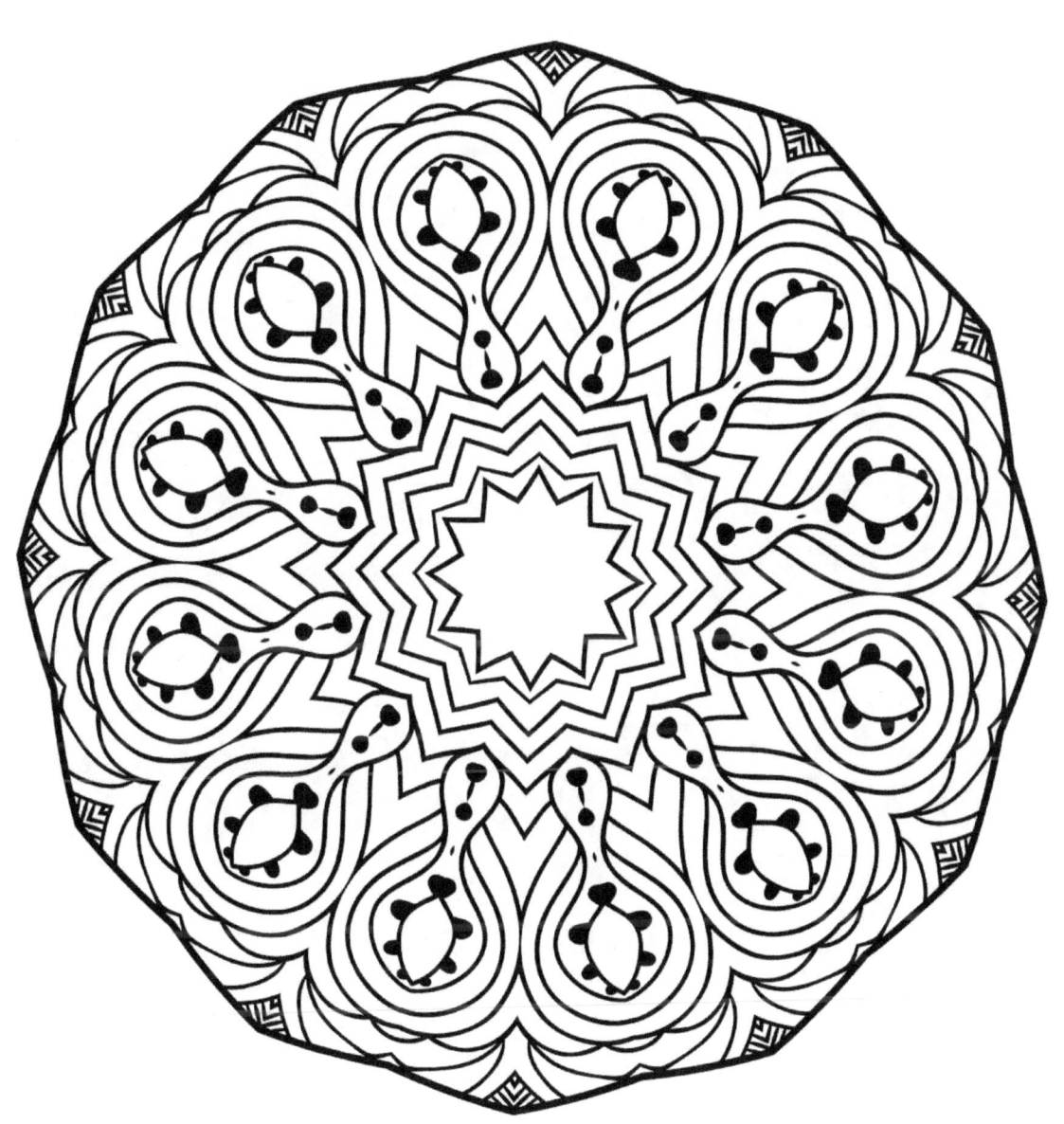

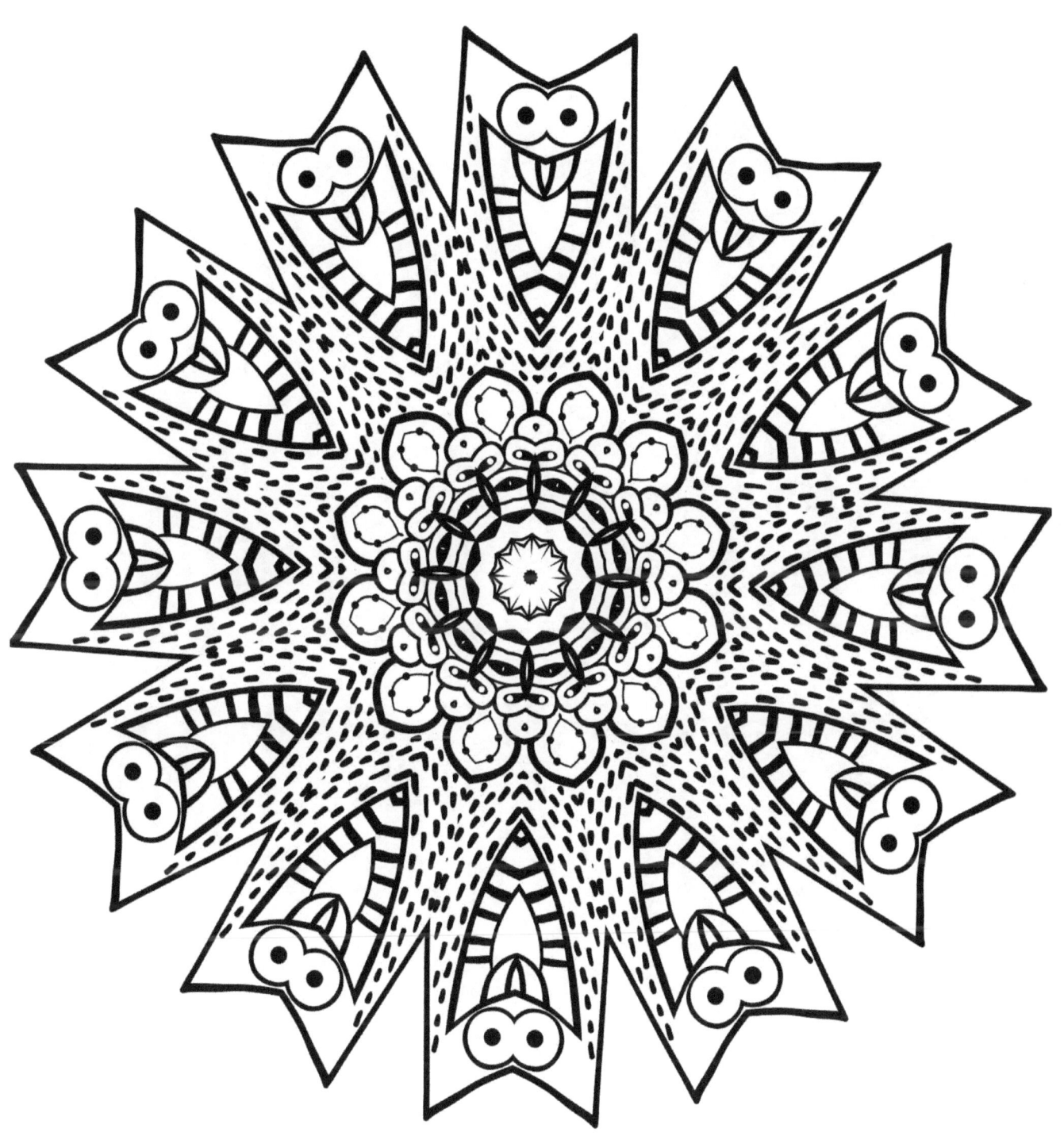

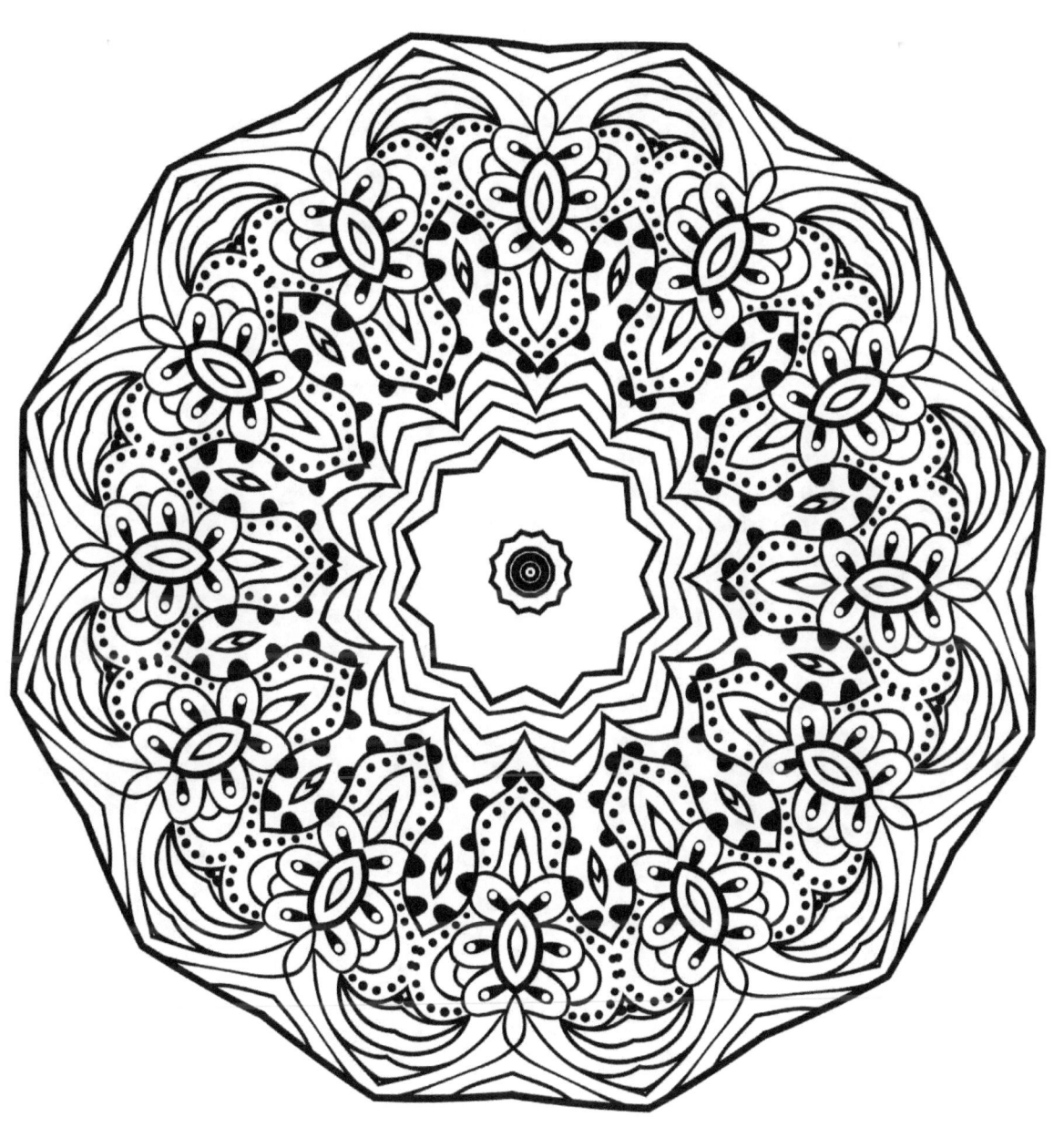

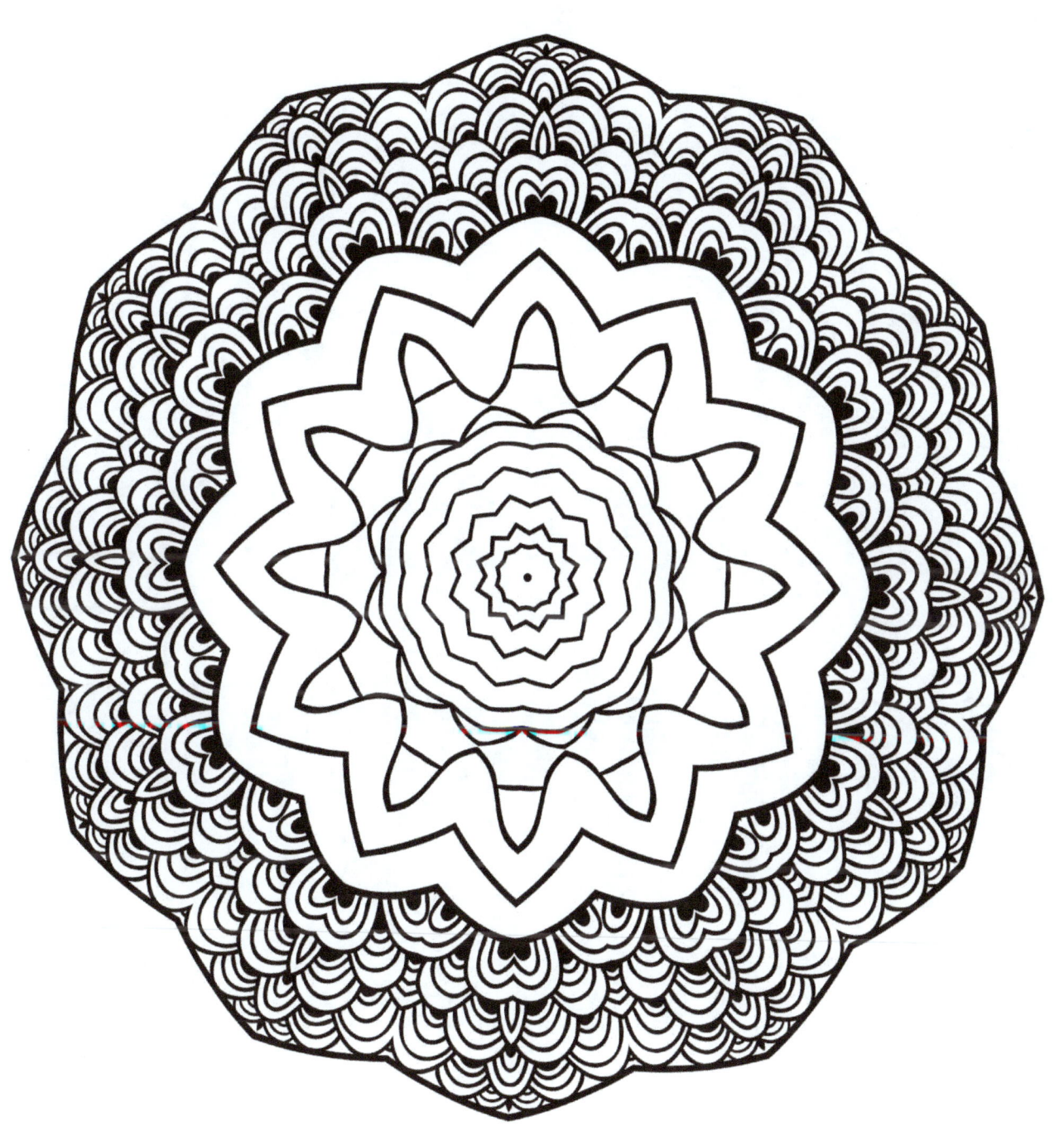

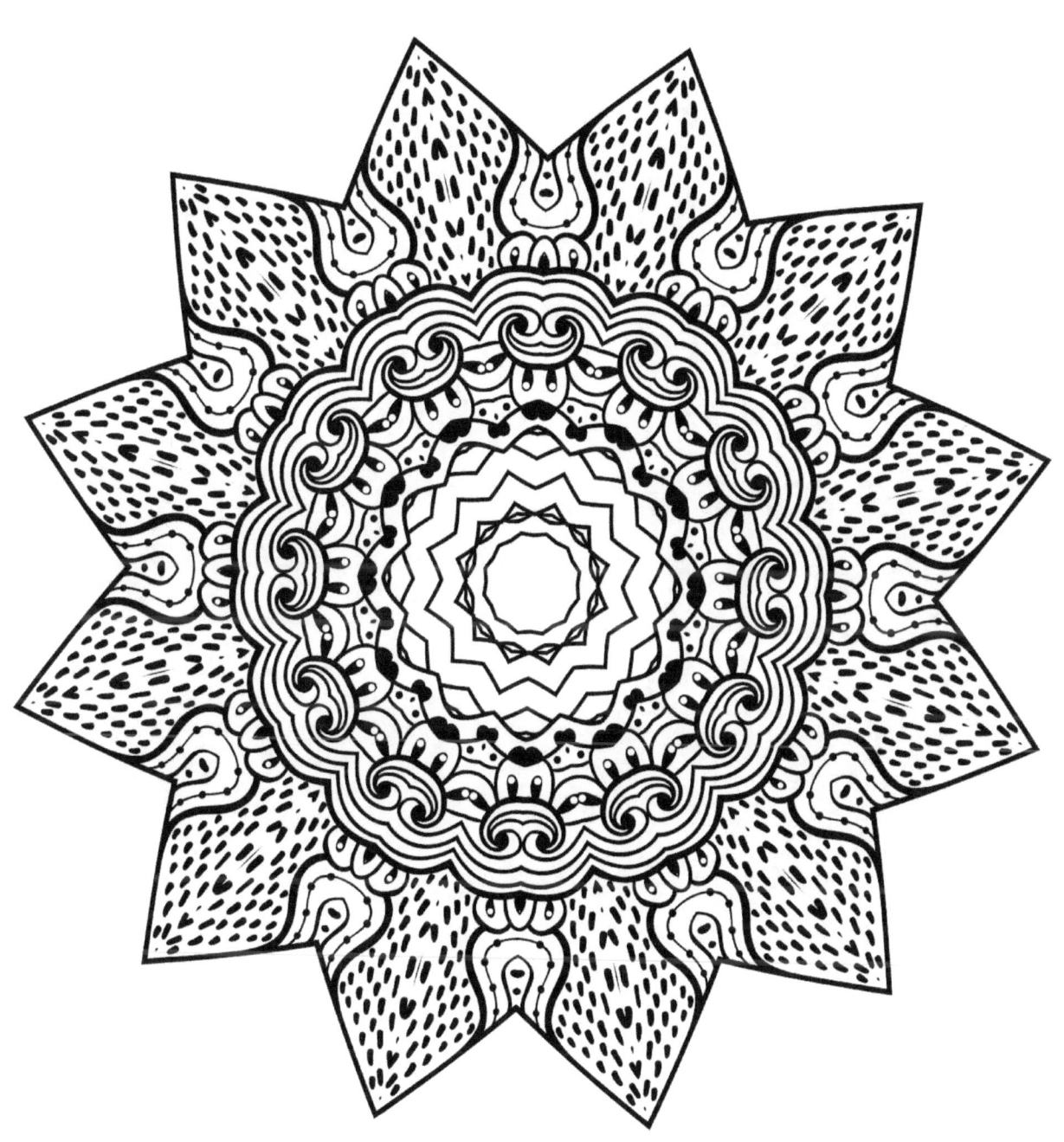

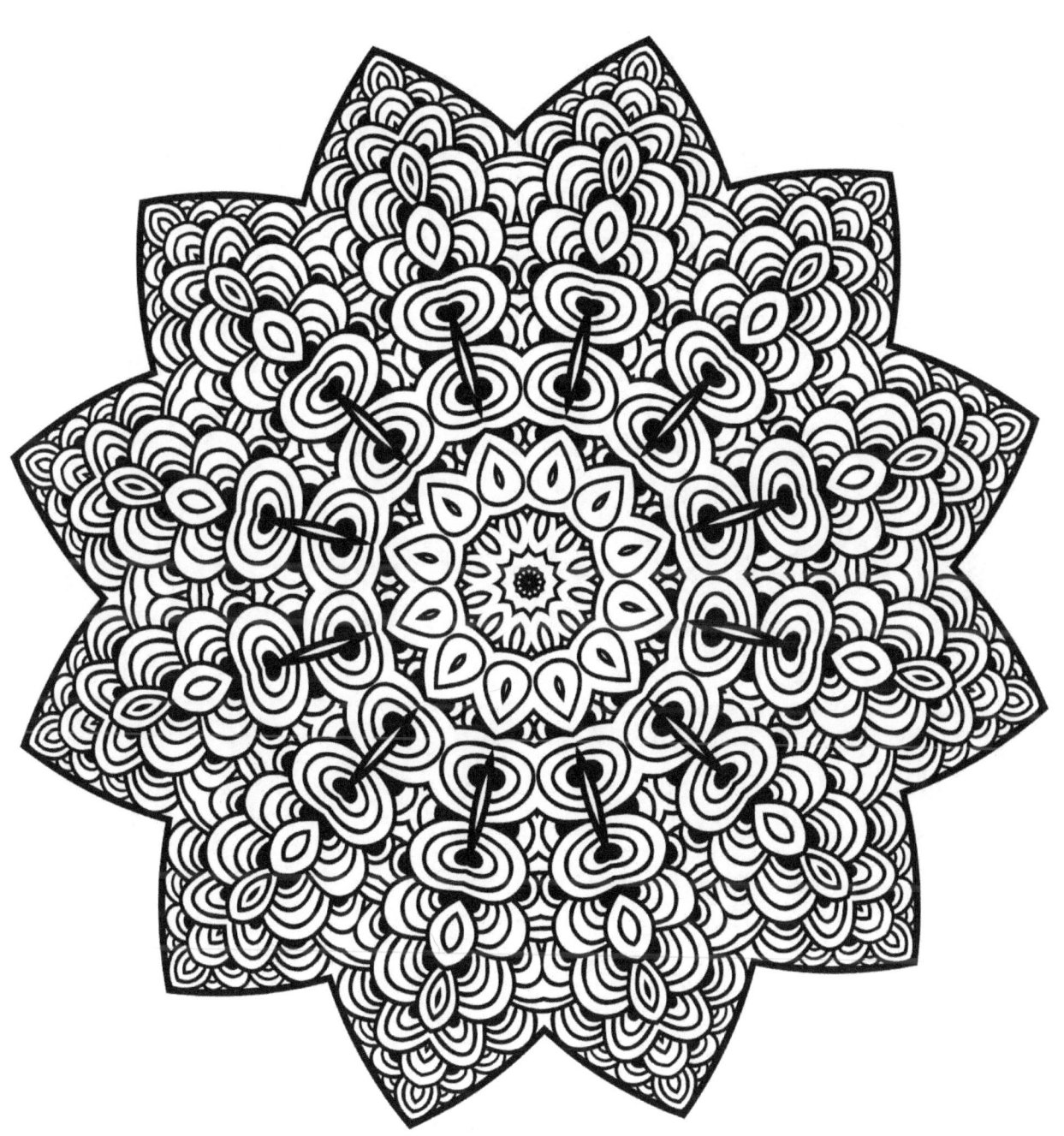

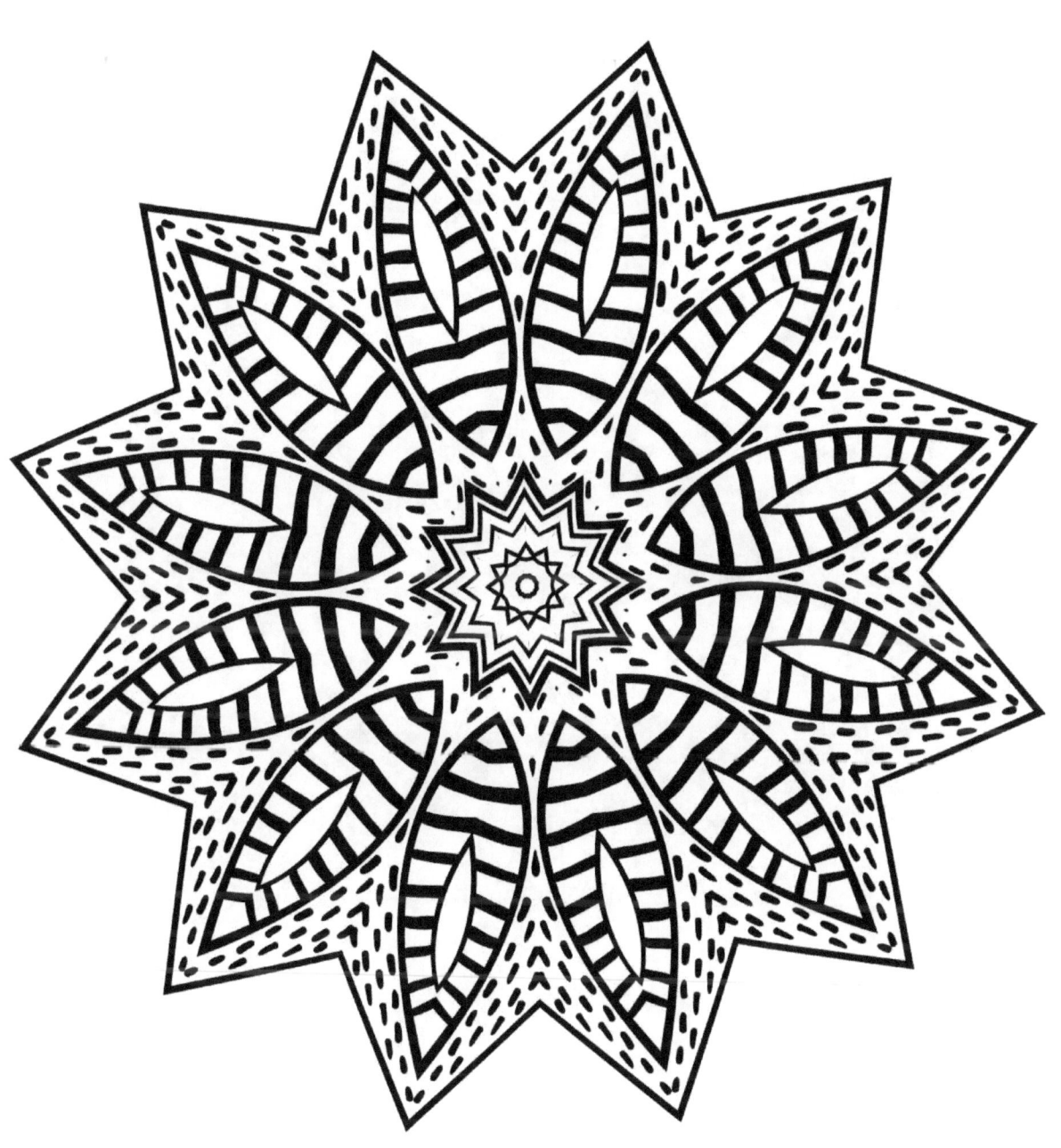

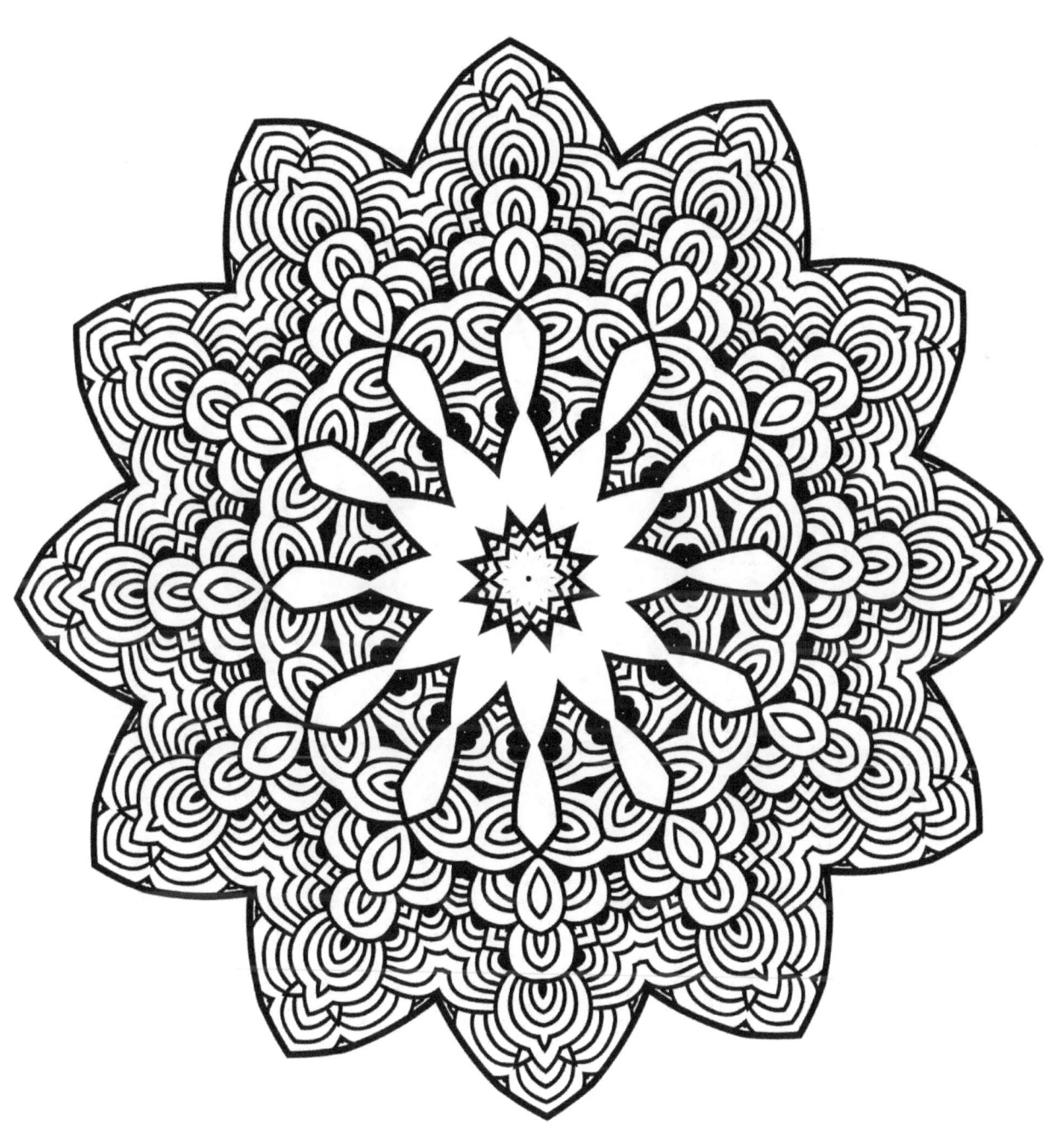

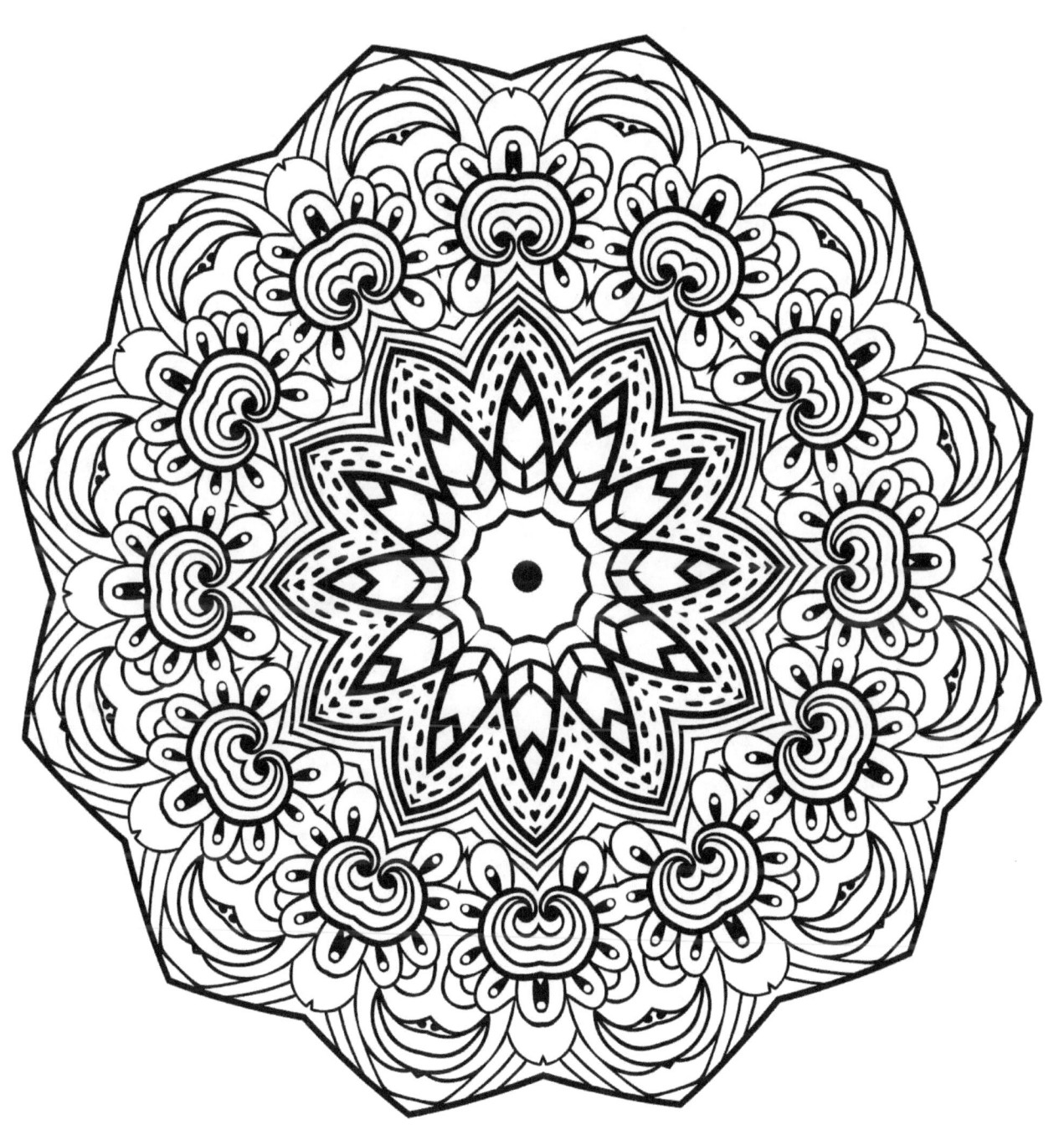

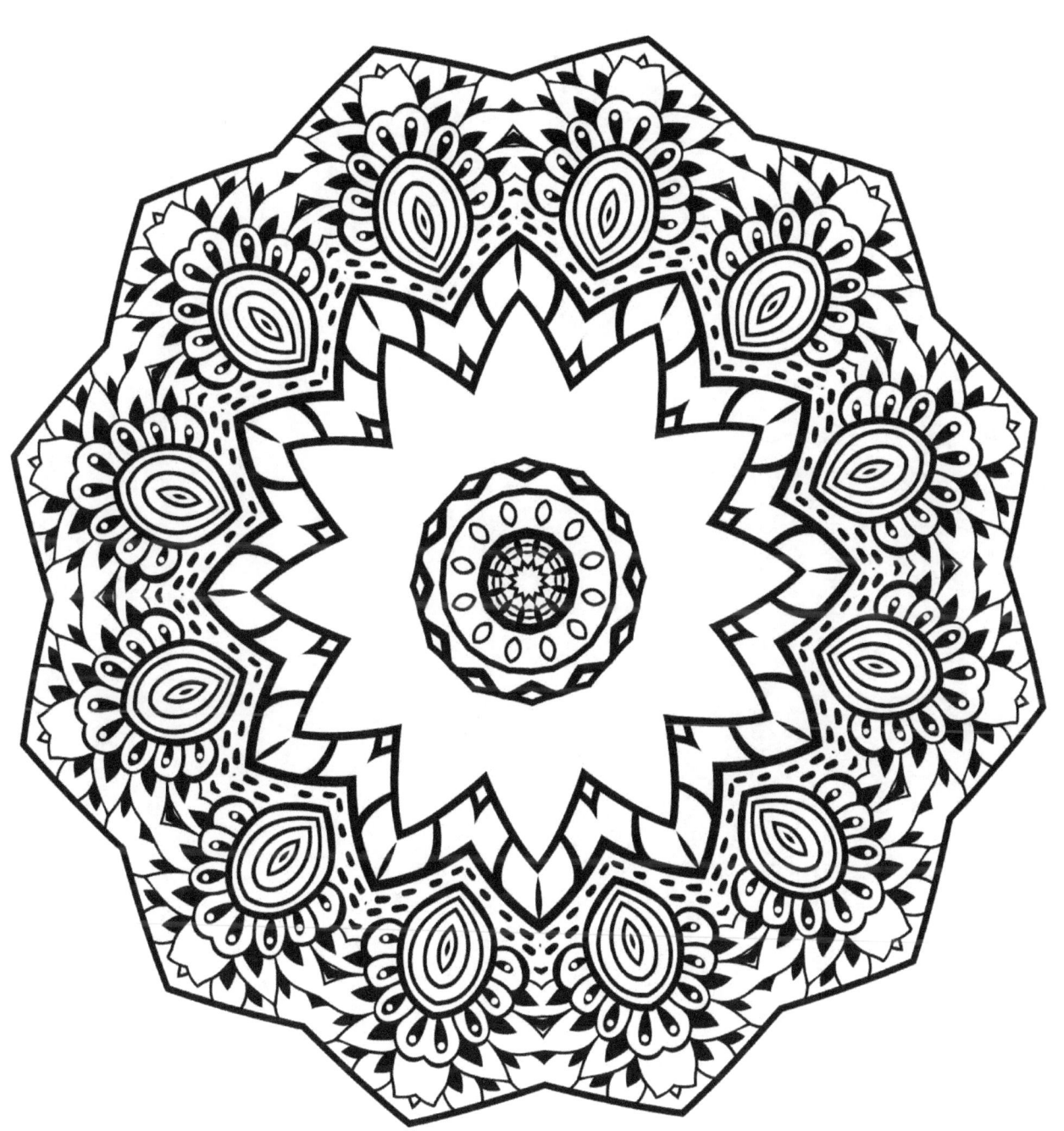

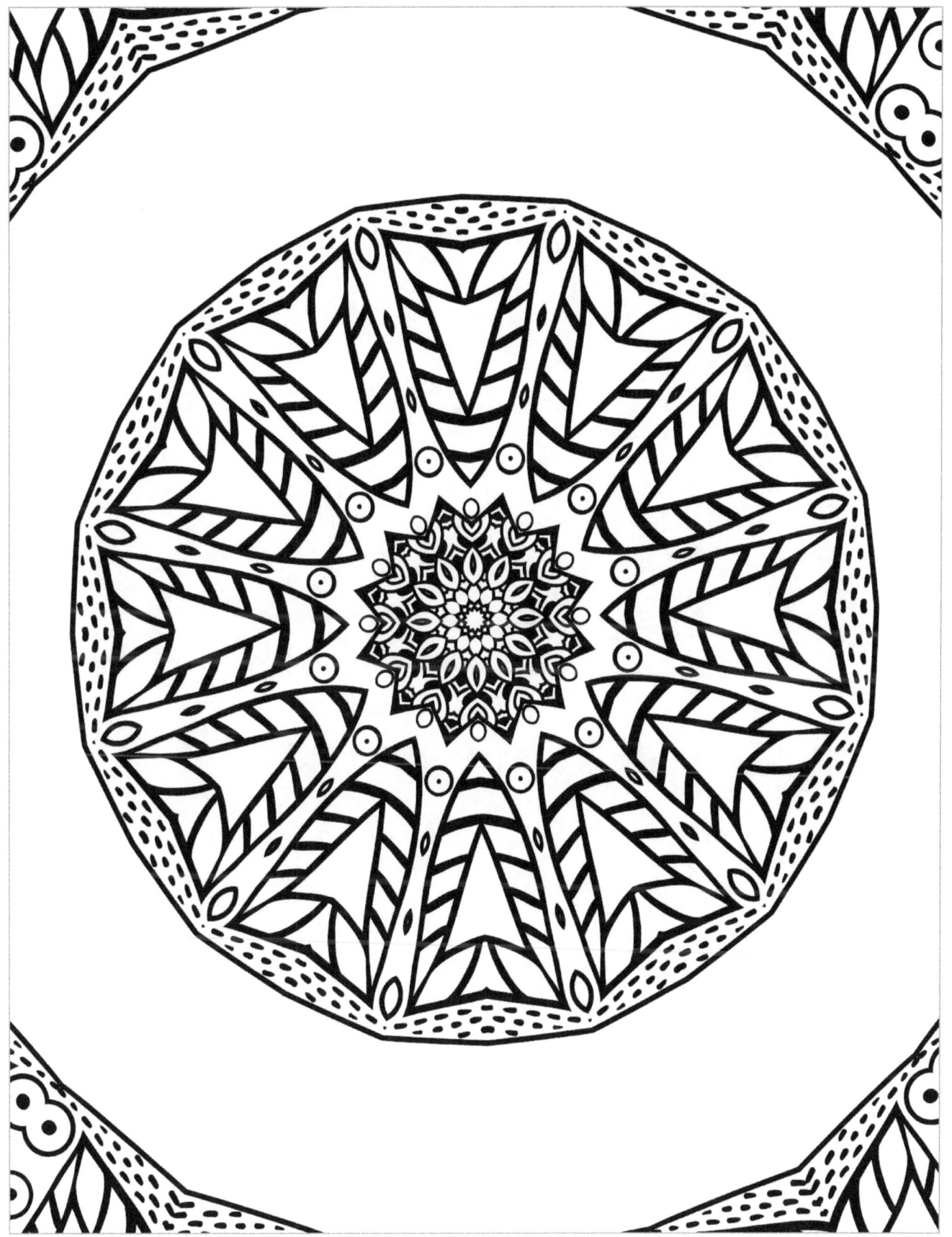

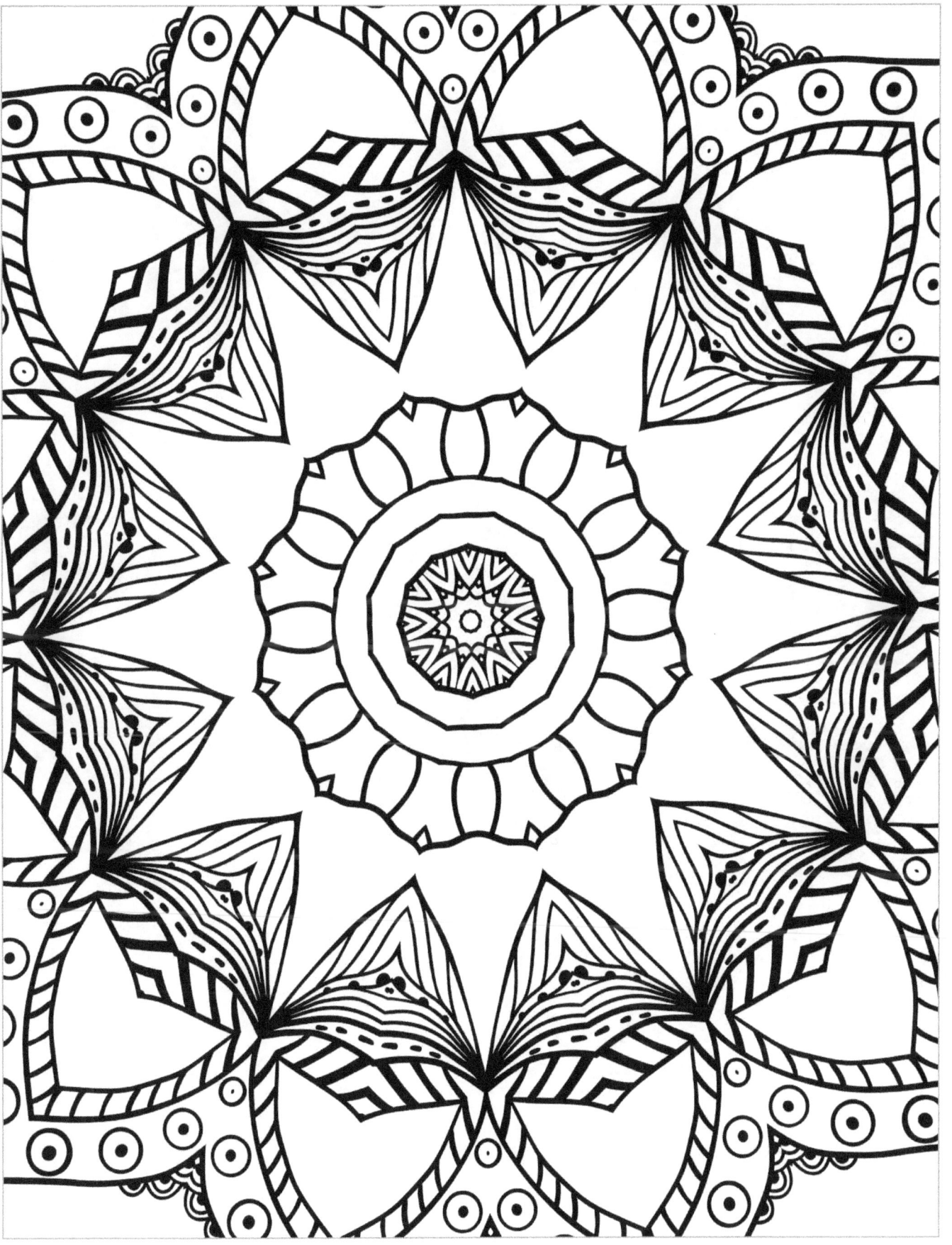

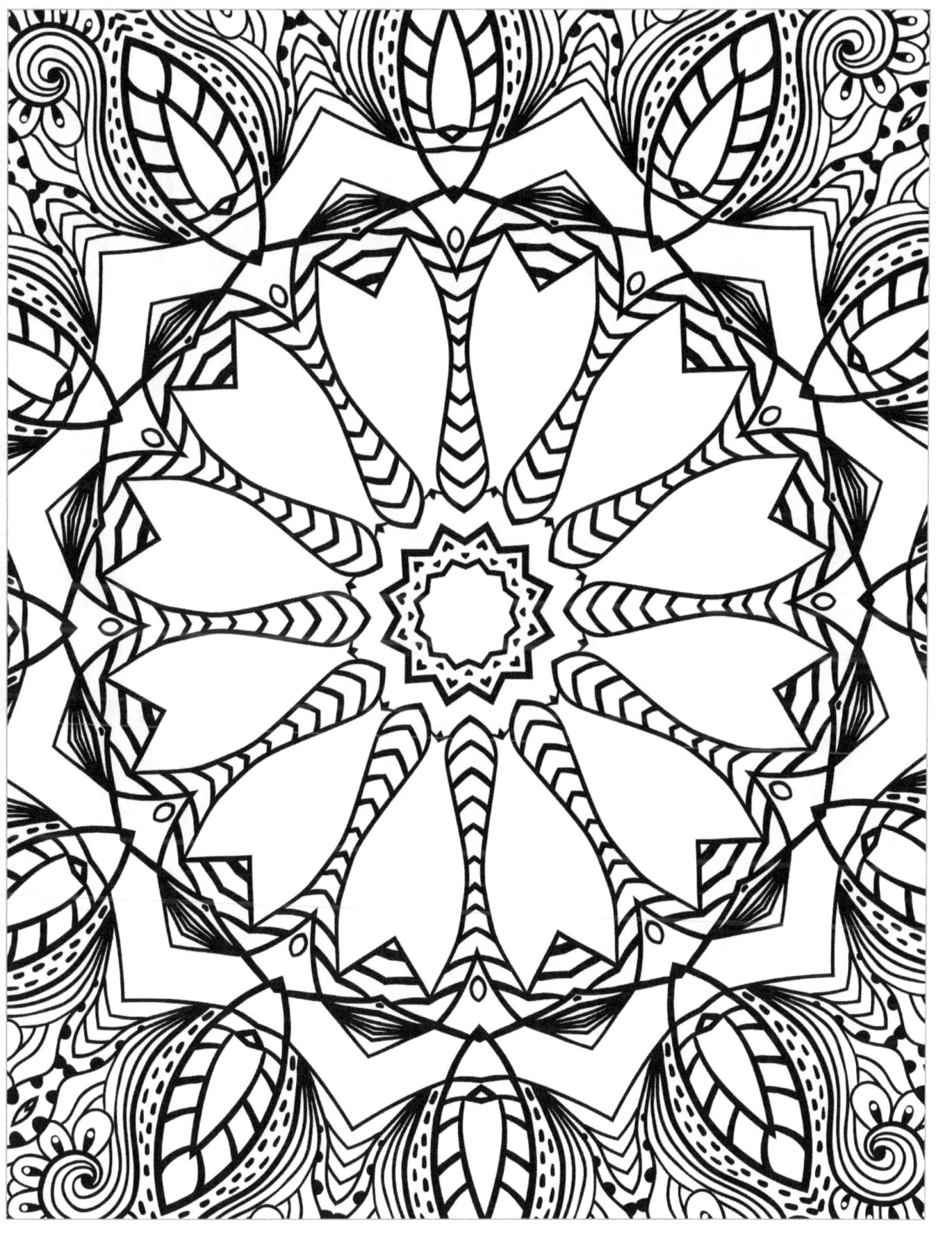

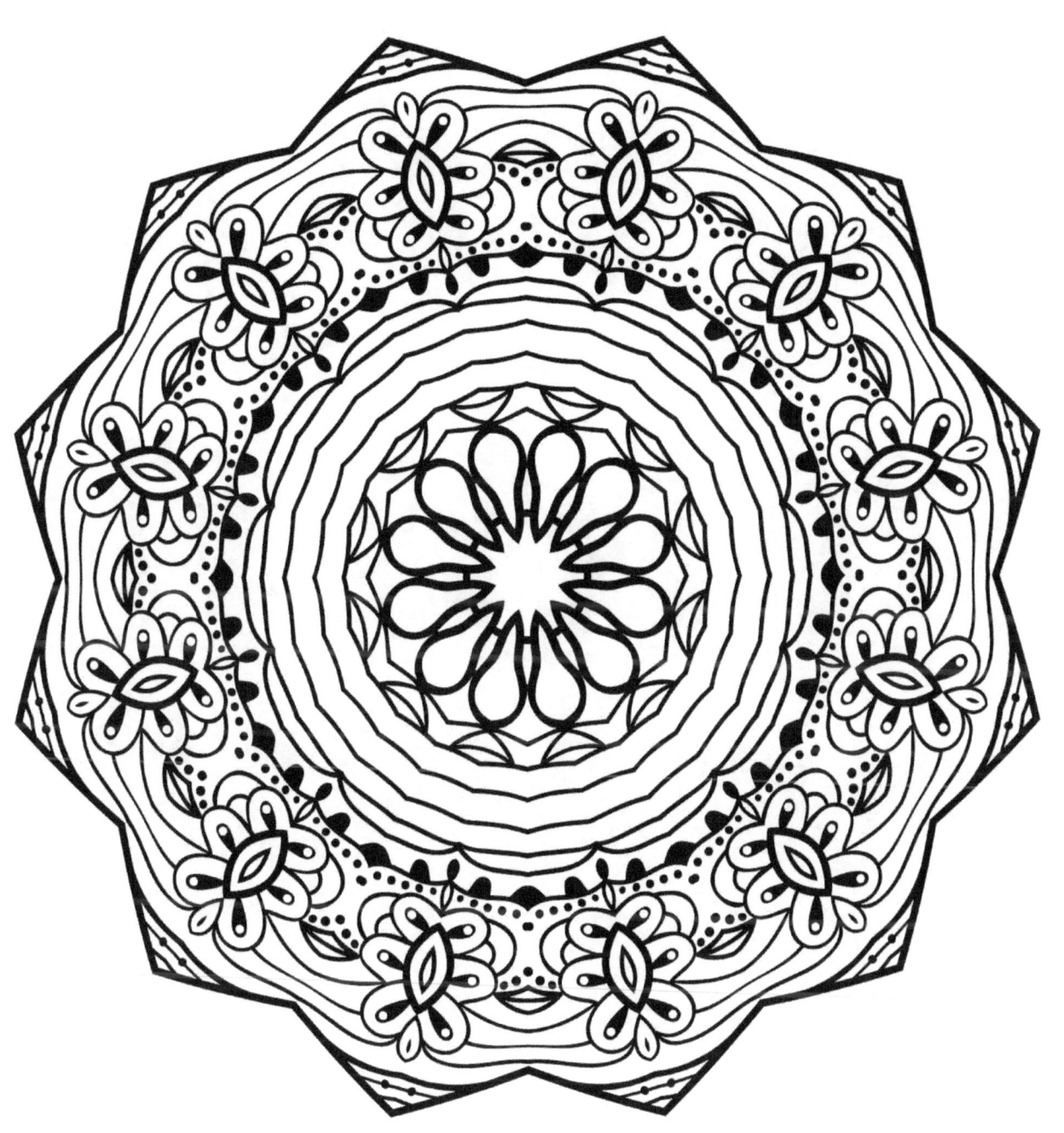

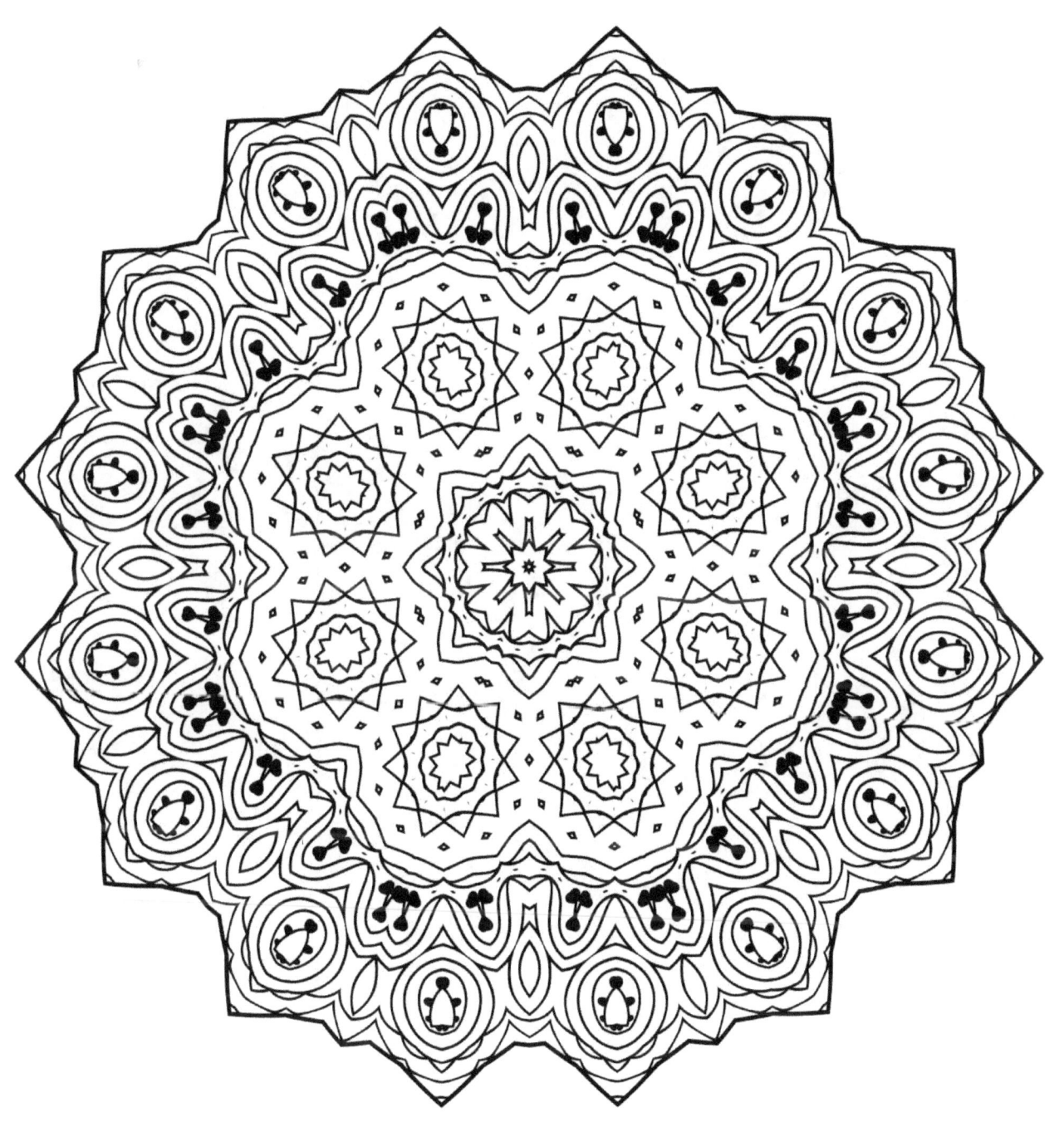

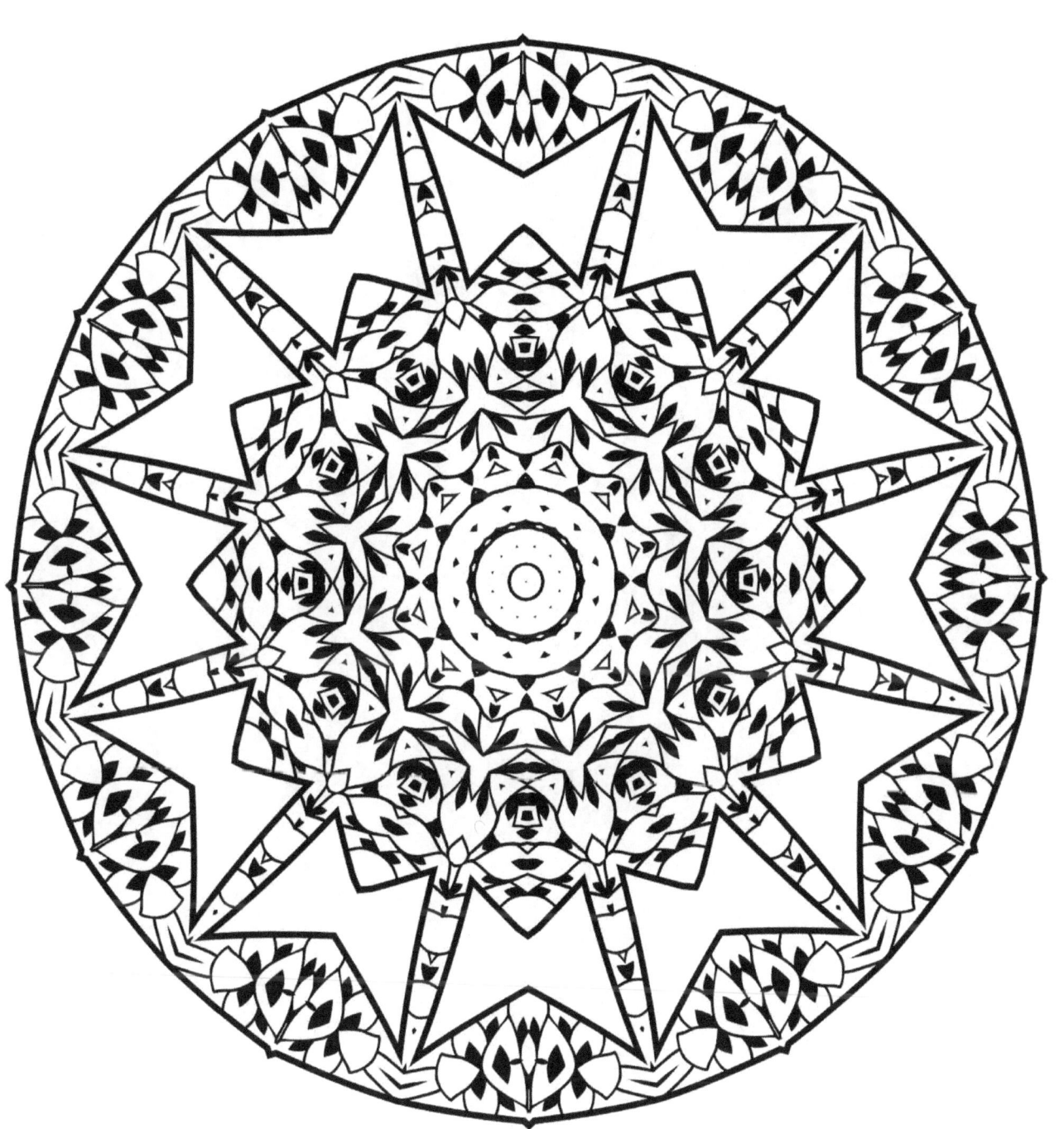

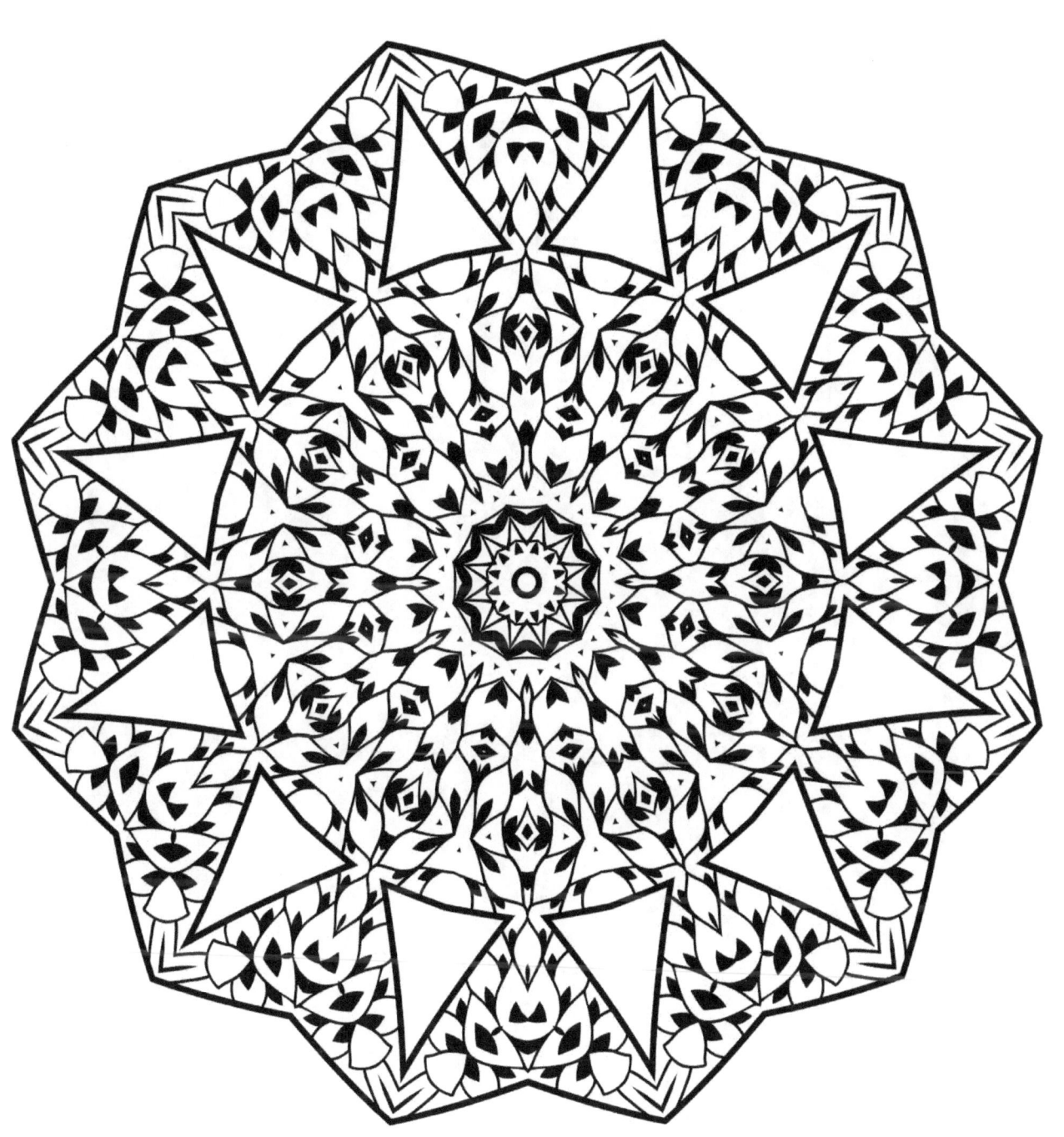

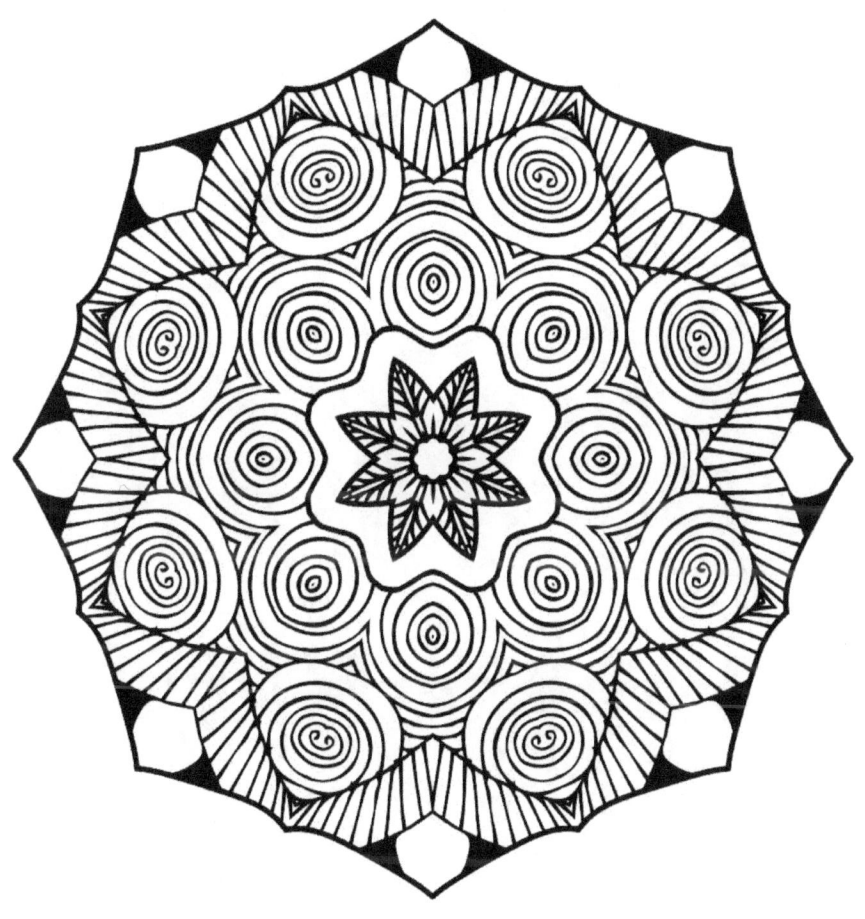

Thank you

www.ingramcontent.com/pod-product-compliance
Lightning Source LLC
Chambersburg PA
CBHW080633190526

45169CB00009B/3378